Third Person... Present Tense

First published in 2025 by Paragon Publishing, Rothersthorpe
© Ian McGaffney 2025

The rights of Ian McGaffney to be identified as the author of this work have been asserted by him in accordance with the Copyright, Designs and Patents Act of 1988.

ISBN 978-1-78792-098-9

Book design, layout and production management by Into Print
www.intoprint.net
+44 (0)1604 832149

Third Person... Present Tense

Ian McGaffney

Third Person ...

For

Ilyana, Ivan, Christian,
Fabiana, Ian, Ivanova, Sebastian, Maria Corina.

Preface

Are we protagonists, participants, or mere observers? Do you ever ask yourself this question?

I'm talking about our personal position (and perception) in and of life, and how we choose to live it. Only each of us can decide whether we actively participate in our individual world or limit ourselves to being silent – but not always innocent – bystanders.

Is there a fine line between these choices? (Perhaps these choices merge at some point.) Or is it that we are able to discern and choose *when* we should jolt ourselves into action, or remain inert, (thus eventually becoming complicit), as disinterested observers, merely watching as the world, *our* world, continues to keep spinning – and it will – with us or without us. Should we leave it in the hands of a third person? Is it *safe* to place it in the hands of a third person?

The poems, or ramblings, presented in this book, are recounting events, observations, fantasies, or dreams, maybe some from the past, from the present, or even of the future.

"One man in his time plays many parts"

- As You Like It, Act 2, Sc. 7

Third Person ...

THINKING

Present Tense

Letters From Home

He would wander
through burnt out forests,
stumbling on charred remains and stumps,
whilst looking up at still smouldering trees, once regal
and gnarled,
now sticklike persons, witnesses to the Devil's deeds,
all carried out in the name of a madman.

The eery silence
only interrupted by the shuffling of his weary gait,
treading softly on a mattress of compressed,
decomposed leaves,
that in places turned into a sludge, oozing a venom
and reeking of rot.
And he continued to roam.

He would dwell on mountains,
revisiting memories,
foraging for morsels to calm his hunger,
and anything to quench his rasping throat, punished
by the visible fumes
swirling around his feet as if he was standing in clouds.

He'd stare out at the barren valleys, the wasted land,
stretching out as far as his eyes could see,
as the sun was obscured by a permanent haze.

He resumed his walk,
painfully aware that he would be travelling
on an unfinished journey.
Now unsure of foot,
the strength drained from him.
Yet, he continued to search
for any companion,
someone to pray with him
during the dark, scary night.

He'd stay awake
until he succumbed, and was swallowed up
by the starless night which enveloped his body,
seeped into his mind, depleted his will,
and destroyed his soul.

The toxic, acrid stench woke him,
invading his senses,
and blinding his eyes.
His body would blister,
and he would scream out in pain.

Laying down again for an eternal rest,
he became aware of the slow, wheezing rise and fall
of his chest.
And he cried, for he knew,
there would be no more.
No more letters from home.

Present Tense

Third Person ...

thinking

– 10 –

A Victim

I suppose,
in a way,
I am an observer
from a distant shore.
Maybe an onlooker,
or even an innocent bystander.
Just possibly guilty
of indolence and neglect.

We are all guilty
of ignorance,
or rather of ignoring
pillage and treason,
which makes us all accomplices,
to acts without reason.

thinking

A Sorry State

You look out through tinted glasses
in the glaring sun.
Yet the tainted vision is all too apparent
as the scales fall away from observant eyes,
watching the gathering storms on the not too distant horizon.
The clouds swaying like masses,
announcing the season,
a change in the air,
for whatever the reason.

The blistering heat
that seals your lips,
as if telling you to not dare pass judgement.

We'd look for some hope
in the faces of forces,
against the perennial dust that has fallen through cracks,
or brushed under the stares,
fuelled by burgers and Coke,
and driven by lust,
in the land of brilliant teeth, and decaying minds,
of false smiles,
of awesome words,
too much appreciation,
and excessive self-gratification.

Present Tense

thinking

Under The Influence

Are they all messengers,
delivering letters
in any form?
Every one
to anywhere,
everywhere.

Or are they empty vehicles
carrying unwilling,
or unwitting, passengers
on endless journeys
into a woven web?

Are they becoming a religion?
Or are they already a religion?
Maybe a cultivated cult
of self-anointed icons?
False idols,
to be worshipped
and rewarded copiously
by deluded followers,
seeking a path to their own relevance,
via revelations
that illuminate their dark, lost world.

Present Tense

thinking

Freedom

Nobody really knows
what happened
behind closed doors,
beyond the half-shut eyes.

Nobody dare see
the searing images,
the burning scars
nor ever stand,
to face the naked truth,
whilst telling brazen lies.

Who could tell,
who would tell
of their basic human needs?
Only offering poor excuses for nefarious deeds.

Who would have thought
that those soaring icons,
converted in stumbling heroes,
are now fallen idols,
left crawling
on their knees.

Present Tense

thinking

Anybody There?

I stand outside,
looking in.
I don't like what I see,
yet I can't do anything about it.
Or maybe I can.

I lie down.
I look up,
then close my eyes.
Darker than dark.
Still points of light,
but where do they lead?
The edges of the night are diffuse.
There are frayed images like that of a lone banner, a standard,
left in tatters.
As if anybody mattered.

I look down
There is an abyss.

thinking

Fallout

You'd stagger through the fallout,
tread easily on the shattered bones,
the broken homes.
Kicking the ashes,
the still warm embers,
envisioning images,
and trying to remember.

You'd try to rebuild places
on burned and barren land,
but never on shifting sand,
or moving mountains
of pure regret,
replacing the foundations,
and trying to forget.

Present Tense

thinking

Mirror

He'd stare
into the distance,
and then up close.
After painstaking
hours of self-reflection,
he'd hear the cracks,
the breaking glass.
The mirrored images
shattering and scattering
in thousands of pieces,
broken and unrecognisable,
covering the floor.

He'd walk,
barefoot,
over those shattered shards.
Bleeding
silently,
and oblivious to pain
no more.

Present Tense

thinking

Mirror, Mirror ... Self-Reflection

One day,
he would look into the mirror.
He would find himself staring hard,
getting up close.
He grew incredulous
at some point,
unable to believe his eyes.
There she was,
staring back at him.

His mind raced as he tried to understand what was happening.
His better half had been there all this time,
he just had not seen her.
Apparently, they had more in common
than that what he thought had been pulling them apart
all this time.
It suddenly dawned upon him
that there appeared
to be so much they shared
without him having realised.

In the past he had always reflected
about how ugly he had grown,
about the person he had become.
Yet now he could see
there was still beauty
he could face, and embrace,
in the future.

He kissed the mirror goodbye,
opened the door to a new world,
and added another dimension to his life.

Present Tense

thinking

ID

I'd walk
in the shadows
of an endless maze,
retracing steps,
treading softly,
not wanting to disturb the surroundings.

I'd fumble,
maybe stumble,
sometimes crumble,
but never fall
under those heavy thoughts
weighing me down
in my constant talks
with my inner self

Yes,
I'd talk.

Present Tense

thinking

Time's Up

Your soul gives in,
your heart gives out.
Your head is confused,
and your mind is in doubt.

Your hands are shaky,
your knees are weak.
Your tongue is tied,
and you can barely speak.

Your eyes are blurry,
your hearing is gone.
Your nose is running,
and you're almost done

Your chest is heaving,
your throat is sore.
You're now full of pain,
and can't take any more.

You're barely awake,
you're cold to the core.
Your number is now up,
and it's ten and three score.

Present Tense

thinking

All Bets Are Off

I'll bet you,
if you dare.
Tell me why you stare,
and tell me that you care,
maybe even share,
some love that you might spare,
from a heart that's really there,
to one that's now laid bare.
Tell me life's not fair,
when there is just a cross to bear.

Present Tense

thinking

Are We Aware?

We are
forged in the past
by malleable minds,
moulded by memories,
able to pick and choose
only what we wish to last.

I may speak the words,
I might proffer a hand
to lay down with me,
side by side,
eyes closed,
and entering a dream
to a promised land.

There would be moments of bliss
and beads of sweat.
Promises sealed with a kiss
as we embark on a voyage
we would never forget,
or maybe even regret.

We'd shake off the past
and try to prevent
remaining in the present,
but rather looking at a future
conditioned with resent.

Present Tense

Third Person ...

thinking

The Present

A surprise package,
a present,
a thought from the past,
and maybe something for the future.

A gift, tied together with glue, sticky tape
and pieces of string,
maybe even some hopes and dreams,
a little piece of everything.

Possibly, it holds a sweater, a jumper, or even an overall.

One size never fits all, it should be made to measure.
It might just be too large and swallow you up,
or you might outgrow it, and discard it, with barely a stare,
even less a thought.

With wear and tear it might become stained, torn
or even ripped apart at the seams,
exposing holes,
baring souls,
which not even a nimble thimble could repair.

Present Tense

Third Person ...

HEALING

Present Tense

Third Person ...

The Third Person

The third person came along,
right out of nowhere.
You never even saw it coming.

It didn't join you for a game of pretence,
and it would laugh at you,
until it made you cry.
You'd keep telling yourself over and over
that what you were living was just a little white lie.

It would leave you sometimes,
but never leave you alone,
no matter how hard you'd try.
It just didn't make any sense
and it left you wondering why.

It would feel its way into your life,
eat its way into your very core,
hardly showing you any feeling,
intent on leaving you reeling,
and making you beg for a suffering no more.

It had its way of talking,
sometimes hardly saying a word,
knowing where to hurt you,
in a way that was previously unheard.
All this time it was assuming
that you had been brought together,
maybe by something even deeper,
a relation that had to be shared.

Present Tense

healing

Who Do You Think You Are!

Maybe you think I am your lover,
but we're not really even friends.
You never could understand,
nor ever lend a helping hand,
and forget about trying to make amends!

Maybe you think it is all over,
when this is just the start.
Deep inside we both know,
that this will just grow and grow,
and you will feast on an ailing heart.

Maybe you think I'll dive for cover,
that I won't want to see you face to face.
You might take me on a ride,
just me and you, side by side,
before you come back over to my place.

Maybe you think I'm worth the time,
but I won't tell you when I've had enough.
In the meantime, we'll just try to get on,
but don't ever try to call my bluff.

Present Tense

healing

Game On

So, nice to see you back.
I knew you'd never leave my side.
This time I'll meet you face on,
I will not hide.
After all, I have too much skin in this game.
I'll try to keep you at arm's length,
and although you try to change your name,
you can try to hurt me as much as you like,
and nothing will ever be the same.
Yes, you have the upper hand.

Present Tense

healing

You Never Left Me

In my heart,
deep down,
I knew it.
I had this uneasy feeling
you never left my side.
It was right,
on the face of it, I felt it.
Those feelings were just waiting to surface,
in some shape or form.

And there you were.
Just hanging around,
all awhile,
biding your time.
You always knew you would never leave me.
Never leave me alone.

You'd gnaw your way back into my mind,
you hurt my feelings,
and you made my skin crawl
with your evil intentions.
I'd chosen to ignore you at my peril.
But you wouldn't give up.
You were here to stay.

Present Tense

Third Person ...

healing

Eating Out

So, all of a sudden
you prefer eating outside.
Did you do it on purpose?
Maybe this way I could see you finally for what you are.
Or is it so you get to spend more time with me?
And there's me thinking you prefer to eat only inside.

So now I get to see you
close up,
first hand,
face to face.
Frankly,
I'm not sure I like what I see.
It frightens me.
You are,
after all,
revolting,
and you know how to get under my skin.

I don't find you attractive in any way,
yet you are attracted to me.
Against my will I might say.

It's strange watching you eat
and see that what I thought held me together
now starts to so easily fall apart.
It has taken time,
though now it takes its toll.
Before I go,
you promise to give me a ring.

Present Tense

healing

Those Cells

Those cells,
so many cells,
awaiting,
and indifferent to their victims.

They have seen so many prisoners,
and at first are unaware of their sentences.
They will soon have their say,
as they eventually decide just how long they will stay.

They will witness what happens
at all times of day:
the injustice,
the starving,
the torture,
the suffering and the pain.

The victims will feel alone,
abandoned with their thoughts,
which keep them awake on their long, dark, endless nights.
Their conditions will be cruel, harsh, and inhuman.
Some prisoners might get off lightly,
even walk away after special treatment,
and good behaviour.

Others will remain,
enduring a life sentence,
whilst wasting away.

Face Up

Some days,
sometimes,
I would just lie there,
as if in a dream.

I could feel the sun
as it burned me within,
taking my life
whilst caressing my skin.

I knew that you had found me,
and I would warm to your touch,
but never ever thinking
it might be just too much.

One day
I'd wake up,
look in the mirror
and start to stare,
finding myself
face to face
with another type of nightmare.

Far away from the harmful glare,
hidden in darkness,
the truth laid bare.
This had developed
into something
much more than a scare.

Another demon to face,
another treatment to chase.
With time running out,
it was almost impossible
to keep up with the pace.

Present Tense

healing

Tinnitus or ...

You called me constantly,
every day,
all the time,
each waking minute,
and especially during those dark, dark nights

That endless ringing
of the siren's call.
I could hear you,
tempting and taunting me,
hunting and haunting me,
until I could take it no more.

I might eventually listen.
After all,
I had no choice
but to become accustomed
to your whining voice.

healing

Wanton Waste

That wasting feeling
the wasting skin
the wasting bones
that lie within.

The wasting cells
taking their prisoners.
The wasting sinews
the wasting of time
that I once knew.
The wasting debt
that was overdue.

The awaiting strife
that uphill fight
making wrongs of right.
Just a show of might
in an endless plight.

That wasted life
just wasting away.

healing

His Dark, Dark Room ... Again

He'd stumble,
once again,
into his dark, dark room.
All alone,
apart from his relentless thoughts
bouncing off the walls,
and reverberating in his head.
All of this together with the unforgiving siren,
slowly driving him mad.

Of course there were demons
feeding off the remains,
gnawing at his conscience,
rubbing at the stains
whilst reviving the past.

He'd crawl into the corners,
searching for slivers of light,
without ever realising
the extent of his plight,
thinking his only chance of redemption
was that forever never lasts.

Present Tense

healing

A Private War

He was his own worst enemy,
facing his foe on his own.
Constantly fighting,
he'd roll up his sleeves,
find a convenient dark corner,
and beat himself up.

Caught on the ropes,
he'd totter and teeter,
and slump to the ground,
unable to envision,
or even think,
of just one more round.

Bruised and battered,
he'd drag himself to his feet,
his confidence now shattered,
his defeat now complete.

Staggering to his corner
he'd seek a few seconds,
take a look at the damage,
and finally decide
that he might be able to manage.

Present Tense

The Quiet Place

He started on a journey,
a journey to the unexpected.

There had been indications
right from the start.
He was slow on the uptake
and misunderstood as not so smart.

It never occurred to him,
until much later,
after red faced moments
and innocent blunders,
with acquiescent nods
at off theme comments,
and asking for repeated words
as if something was missing.
It all sounded so odd,
and confusing.

He still had his voice
and a sharp-tongued wit,
with a rapid riposte
that came more from a thought
than an answer to a question.

Vacant stares,
or a slight movement of the head,
when it had nothing to do
with that being said.

He followed a subtle reading of lips
and always used subtitles to see
where he was being led.

The ringing started
in a tunnel,
at the pealing of bells.
An unforgiving siren
appeared at the gates,
leading the way
to a descent into hell.

The unceasing cacophony
was an unwelcome companion,
even on a visit with friends
to enclosed spaces.
Their lack of understanding
of what was gradually happening,
was now so apparent
on all of their faces.

He became accustomed to the semi-isolation
whilst a blank look filled his face.
The signs showed the way
to the silence that was his destination,
the end of the road,
in a quiet, lonely, place.

Present Tense

healing

It Is

It is.
It is what it is,
but you can call it what you like.
And it's here to stay.
It will take over your life,
find a way into your mind,
and one thing you will notice,
it will never be kind.
Little by little, piece by piece,
it destroys all that it finds.

Maybe one day,
AI will overtake it
and drive it away.
Then there will be
just nothing left to say.

A new wind has arrived,
and will blow it away.
That's just how it is.

Present Tense

Third Person ...

FEELING

Present Tense

Third Person ...

Common Ground?

You probably thought
it was common ground.
A place where love and reason
were soon to be found,
offering solace
with enticing words,
and their comforting sound.

You felt safe
in the warmth of an extended hand
that touched the fibres
and aroused the senses,
yet made you feel
you were in no man's land.

Present Tense

That Dark, Dark Room

He would crawl back into that dark room.
No windows,
just walls that seemed to close in,
as if trying to squeeze the life from him.

He had dragged in his assorted baggage,
overflowing with broken dreams,
some nightmares, and memorabilia,
a few moments from the past.

He would rummage through all of these reminders,
not knowing what he was really looking for.

He would stare off into the dark,
an abyss of unending depth, and would start to peer,
as if trying to penetrate that inky void.

Was it the blackness of his soul?

He saw demons dressed as ghosts,
coming and going in his head,
trying to confuse him with events that might have been,
or with words he may have never said,
maybe even of images he long thought dead.

The vivid scenes came fast, many fleeting, some lingering
in his thoughts.
He wanted to confront anyone – or anything –
that came to mind.

He would punish himself more than his imaginary foe,
and end up wasted and wretched,
lying on the cold floor,
surrounded by shattered visions, strewn around him
like old pieces of clothing, rags even,
torn apart at the seams.

Third Person ...

feeling

The Intruder

He stumbled through the stolid trees,
his feet dragging at the fallen leaves.
He searched to find the way,
a possible new direction,
or even some purpose for his journey.

Maybe he had already arrived but didn't know it.
Possibly he was really lost, beyond saving even.
He realised what was happening to him,
despite his feeling devoid of any emotions most of the time.

Nevertheless, occasionally, an overwhelming sadness would
descend on him,
wrapping itself around him,
squeezing until he found it hard to breathe,
whilst he heard the increasing beat of a thumping heart
that was no longer buried in his chest.

Those constant feelings of despair convinced him
of his advance to nowhere.
Just a never ending circle,
possibly a spiral down to darker places,
to the quiet rooms, secluded spaces to forget the faces,
and finally,
erase all the traces.

Present Tense

feeling

Me And People ... People And Me ...

How many people am I?
How many people are me?
How many people am I supposed to be?
How many people I suppose I should be?
How many people must I be?
How many people I have to be?
Is it really so hard to be just *me*?
Will somebody, something, sometime, just let me be?
Or let me be me?
Maybe some people even set me free?
Maybe I'm wrong,
and it's how it should be.
Just maybe.

Third Person ...

feeling

3D – Another Dimension

I run into them
almost every day.
No, that sounds wrong.
I mean that I meet them often.
Or is it that they follow me around?
They are just waiting
for the right moment
to worm their way into my head.
They run around, upending my world,
throwing things about, creating chaos in every corner,
leaving behind a wake of destruction...
They leave me tired,
exhausted,
drained of all direction ... lost in a fog that takes days to clear.
Yes,
those dark days of demons are something
I fear.

feeling

No Escape

The hungry demons,
those little devils.
The intensive pangs,
the sharpest of fangs,
gnawing at the cables that connect us,
or through the very fibres of our soul.

To what intent?
To inflict pain?
To make us scream
at a broken dream,
or erase the darkest stain
from something that could linger, fester, and remain?

Present Tense

feeling

Wish List

Sometimes,
he wishes.
He wishes he could close his eyes,
wander into that dark room,
and shut down all the motors.
Throw the switches,
deaden the sensors,
erase the thoughts,
shrug off the feelings,
shed himself of memories,
of heavy weights.
Remove the shackles,
break loose the chains,
and free himself from pain.

He wishes.

Sometimes.

Present Tense

Third Person ...

feeling

Slippery Slopes

He would slip back into his dark room,
hide in the corners,
scratching at the rough surfaces
until the tips of his fingers bled,
looking for a stone to hide under,
a rock to hide behind
something to protect himself
from his own demons,
fighting among themselves
to rip him apart,
and eat his bleeding heart.

Present Tense

feeling

Deep Down

He'd travel down to the darkest depths,
holding his breath as if frozen in time.
Moving in slow motion treading the water
and feeling the cold.
He had no idea what he looked for in those icy waters.
Maybe he had lost something, maybe some piece of mind
that had slipped through his hands,
and ended up lying on those shifting sands.

Third Person ...

feeling

Hermit

One day,
just one day,
he'd crawl out from under his rock.
He'd shed his shell,
that empty space
he once called home.

He'd move warily on the shifting sands,
testing the waters as he reached out for other hands,
until eventually realising
that he was all alone.

He'd feel in awe of the open spaces,
the fading faces,
that were beyond his touch.
Yet he again could feel
it was already too late
to ever think
about changing places.

Chastened,
he hastened back,
returning to his natural habitat,
the dark place where he felt most secure,
never to think again
of venturing out,
to a distant, unknown shore.

Present Tense

feeling

What If?

What if
If only
He could
Should he
Would he
Why?

What if
He's lonely
Sad
Bad
Mad
Try?

What if
The only
Way
Say
May
Die?

If not
What then
When
Then
Why
Lie?

What if?

Present Tense

Third Person ...

feeling

Hope

Sad would be the day
that hope departed.
Maybe it would take flight to open skies,
or board a ship in the night to distant shores,
taking everything with it.
Even all of those feelings,
that you thought were just yours.

Nevertheless,
you'd hold on to your dream,
like a kid with a kite,
that's dipping and diving
whilst you put up a fight.

You would never let go,
and would keep that dream in your head,
as you lay in your bed,
facing another sleepless night.

feeling

Insomnia

So, I'm in a nightmare.
One of those stormy nights
with those clouded thoughts,
and an endless torrent
rushing through the already muddied waters.

Breathing deeply, holding it in,
counting the seconds of tensing muscle,
discharging any negative energy,
and hoping to cleanse the toxic waste, expulse the venom
that's eating away
at the very fibre,
that somehow holds you together.

You can almost hear the gnawing,
the constant sound that torments your mind.
Where, and when, will the dam finally burst,
to expulse all the waste,
the remains of that rotting core?

Until you find freedom,
a place from where it can do you harm no longer,
no more.

Present Tense

Third Person ...

DREAMING

Present Tense

Third Person ...

On The Other Side

One day
I'll see you,
on the other side.
Walking in fields of endless lavender,
a shimmering image
in the summer's haze.
Dressed in billowing white linen
that moves like a cloud,
in the gentle warm breeze.

That day,
I'll decide
to follow your path,
on the other side.

I'll walk in the lavender
and breathe the soothing scent,
reaching out for a ride
on the cloud that will lift me,
then bring me to my knees.

Present Tense

dreaming

You

I look for you.
Suddenly you appear out of nowhere.
I see you,
in passing strangers,
in different places.

I imagine you alone,
and then I imagine us,
in a thousand thoughts
of countless scenes on infinite journeys.

I can feel that sensation,
maybe even touch it.
So very real,
so very happy,
yet truly sad.
A guilt-fuelled dream,
that drives me mad.

Present Tense

Third Person ...

dreaming

Reverie

Come,
float with me.
In the sea of dreams.
Close your eyes,
contemplate the stolen heart that rests in a sunken chest.
Travel with me,
and see the world through my eyes.
Feel the warmth of a rising sun, as you accompany me
walking on shifting sands, the crystal water dripping
from searching hands.

dreaming

There They Are ...

They are
consenting adults,
unlikely partners,
yet willing participants,
maybe even victims,
and slaves to their dreams.
Might this turn into a nightmare
in the eye of the storm
in which they'd dance?

They are
drawn together
and torn apart.
Bruised and beaten,
huddled tightly,
seeking refuge,
whilst they ride out the weather,
and taking a chance.

They are
searching for something,
maybe deep down in their soul,
hidden from onlookers
when out of control,
risking their skin
feeling whatever within,
and all for the sake of romance.

Present Tense

dreaming

Falling Together, Falling Apart

They searched for solace
in each other's arms.
Those protective arms,
the shared embrace
of the lover's charms.

Then falling together,
hard and fast,
into the abyss of pleasure,
and oblivious to the harm,
whilst living together
those moments to treasure.

The affairs of the heart,
separated by time,
by too few hours or minutes
and just never enough.
So difficult to prevent
those affairs of the heart
from falling apart.

Present Tense

dreaming

Clouds In The Sky

Why is it that the sunniest of faces
can suddenly turn
into the darkest of places?
Is anybody able to fathom the depths
of those aquamarine eyes
as they change from calm waters
into storm heavy skies?

How can the kind
turn the world on its head,
without bearing in mind
the weight of the words
they sometimes have said?

How can the mood swing
like a metronome
not missing a beat,
but now disrupting the rhythm
by changing their tune?

Present Tense

dreaming

Should I

If you fail,
if you fall,
then fall into my arms.
They are reaching out to save you,
save you from any harm.

Should I fail,
should I fall,
embrace me once more,
one last time,
and feel the hearts beating within.
Then let me go,
free yourself,
run from it all.

Don't try to keep me.
There will be other sunrises to lead you to a different path,
and the sunrays will keep you warm
on a cold, cold day.

Yet, never forget the bond,
never forget those moments,
and remember the words:
Nobody will ever love you this way.

Present Tense

Third Person ...

dreaming

Then What?

Then, there are no words left.
They have all been used up in pointless points,
and inane garble.
Banal conversations,
so shallow that you could drown in them.
They are nothing, yet mean anything, and everything.
Does a raised voice give reason
more meaning?
Does lack of thought,
or empty words,
signify there is no sense,
or any excuse for believing?

Present Tense

dreaming

Mind Your Grammar

It wasn't a full stop,
just a pause,
though maybe indefinite.
No exclamation, nor question,
mark my word!
The subject had made me her object.
She was the definite article in every aspect
and was not too difficult to be consonant with.
She had a way with verbs, and was very verbose.
I found it difficult to find an adjective to describe her, but she
was renowned for having a voice which could go on infinitely.
She was a real case, but we seemed to complement each other,
although she was at times too possessive.
Her love was unconditional, but it was imperative that
in the future it would be conditional.
Or is it already a life sentence?

Present Tense

Word Salad (or Fruit And Nuts?)

She spoke with Okra Quincy at the Waldorf,
ignoring Brussels as words sprouted from her mouth.
Supported by political has beans, even a couch potato,
who sometimes drove her around in his Courgette,
something he would eventually regret.

In case there was a leek
she was forbidden to speak,
cos she had more radishal views.
Shoots spring from her mouth
with a beat trying to take root,
whilst trying to be as American as apple pie – but rather
sounding real corny.

She was cherry picking interviews and unable to stop mixing
apples and pears,
only bringing a word salad to the table.
A convinced advocate being in favour of the greens,
trying to figure it out in an effort to appease.
She came back to earth like a burnt out rocket,
driving people bananas, nuts; a real basket case.

Acting with celerity, smooth as oil with vinegary comments,
taking every opportunity to disparag us, cos that's how she is.
But it was all window dressing,
and we're not talking of peanuts here.
Everything she said was all Greek to me, or was it Romaine?
Anyway, give unto Caeser his due,
she was peppering her opponent, going easy on the balsam,
orzo I thought.

But an advance took place and called her trumps.
The guy knows his onions and squashes her with facts,
leaving her without mush room.
Just watch this man go!

She thought that she'd Waltz into the White House
but her cucumber's up.

Lettuce pray.

Present Tense

Dire Traits… 20/20 Vision

Biden
Hiding
Biding
Chiding
Wheeling
Dealing
Lying
Stealing
Sliding
Slipping
Mumbling
Bumbling
Fumbling
Jumbling
Stumbling
Crumbling

Trump
Trumping
Troubling
Trampling
Tweeting
Trolling
Tolling
Taking
Trying
Faking
Lying
Joking

Poking
Provoking
Stoking
Woking
Arming
Alarming
Charming
Disarming
Defying

Senile
Senate
Speaking
Reaching
Teaching
Preaching
Leeching
Beseeching
Impeaching

Putin

Present Tense

dreaming

Apocalypse

Clever quips
Trembling lips
Simple zips
Shaking hips
Apocalypse

Present Tense

Acknowledgements

Many thanks to Anne and Mark at Into Print for their usual support, assistance, and above all, patience, in the presentation of this *Third Person...Present Tense.*

About the Author

Ian was born on December 17th, 1951, in Liverpool, UK, and emigrated to South America in 1974, where he lived for over 40 years. He is retired and has been living in Madrid since 2016. He has three children and five grandchildren.

Ian McGaffney's other books include:

Dear Cancer, With love... poems expressing the thoughts and feelings of a man with cancer. Raw, personal and uncompromising, *Dear Cancer, With love...* aims to help others who find themselves reeling after hearing that they, or someone they know, has been diagnosed with cancer.

Life, and so on... Observations, reflections, musings, in rhythm with the pendulum of life.

Pensamientos...en otras palabras... Poems in Spanish.

Just a Moment... of Time: a reflection on past and present times.

Present Tense